WOLVES

A COLLECTION OF POEMS
BY JIM JOHNSON

MINNESOTA VOICES PROJECT NUMBER 57

NEW RIVERS PRESS 1993

The publication of *Wolves* has been made possible by generous grants from the
Jerome Foundation and the Metropolitan Regional Arts Council (from an
appropriation by the Minnesota Legislature). Additional support has been pro-
vided by the First Bank System Foundation, Liberty State Bank, the National
Endowment for the Arts (with funds appropriated by the Congress of the United
States), the Star Tribune/Cowles Media Company, the Tennant Company Foun-
dation, the United Arts Fund, and the contributing members of New Rivers Press.
New Rivers Press also wishes to acknowledge the Minnesota Non-Profits
Assistance Fund for its invaluable support.

New Rivers Press books are distributed by:

The Talman Company   Bookslinger
131 Spring Street, Suite 201 E-N   2402 University Avenue West
New York NY 10012   Saint Paul MN 55114

Wolves has been manufactured in the United States of America for New Rivers
Press, 420 N. 5th Street/Suite 910, Minneapolis, MN 55401 in a first edition
of 1,200 copies.

CONTENTS

THE CROSSING

Coming to America
in the dark hold of a wooden ship
that rose and fell
with the swelling of the Atlantic
were mice
eating of the green sickness
in a light that broke
through the rigging
          the cracks in the planks, and
men and women
in dark cloth
crossing and recrossing
themselves.

RUNE

What a man carved
from what was at hand
black ash or birch,
what he tamped
against a frozen chopping block
(it was December, no snow on the ground),
what was wedged
snug inside
what was the head: double-bitted
rusty
dull
and chipped, what he honed
until an edge began to shine —
blacksteel and treeline.

THE UNCUT FOREST

Leave your homeland.
live in a cabin made of logs,
a smoke hole in the roof,
slit windows covered
with skins.
the snow deep, the winter long.
carve your fear
the shape of the wood in mind.
from the forest make what you need,
can't afford to waste.
eat bark bread.
from a spruce log
carve a wooden spoon, use it.
the history of Finland
the history of Finland, Minnesota.

The History of Finland, Minnesota

Always there is coffee and
that day
Emma Leskinen,
scarf like the old country
about her head,
shawl knitted from yarn
spun from dog hair
about her shoulders,
walked along the gravel
edge of the road
and looked up.

                      finally
the railroad laid down its tracks
and built a station
and the painter having finished
painting the station house white
wondered
      what name do I paint
upon this gable?

the nights were warm.
the blueberries blossomed
among the green bush
duff and outcropped rock,
and the pines lived in the wind
when she said *Finland.*

HOMESTEADERS

From the old photographs
we know they never smiled,
their lives stiff
with smallpox, early winters, and rocks.
or they heard the forest
grow beneath their feet.
first they built a sauna,
lived in it
until the logs had dried
and a proper house was hewn.
in their time
they rebuilt the sauna.
the old became, perhaps, a chicken coop.
I remember when I walked among
tall birches and came to
what was once a clearing.
among the new growth
a building remained,
its roof collapsed.   inside
a mirror strung with cobwebs
and framed with a dark-aged wood
hung on the wall.
it reflected the young popple
continuing on.
it was like a wooded pond.
while on the floor
were feathers and scat:
another possibility.

LASKIAINEN (MIDWINTER FESTIVAL)

In a whipsled, down a hill, iced last night,
    the farther you go
    the taller your crops will grow.
the more manure the men haul out onto the ice
    the sooner winter will end.
the women are forbidden to spin yarn
    now that it is Lent
    or spring will never show.
on Shrove Tuesday you heard the cowbells in your head.
    if you hear the owl call
    it will be time to go.

AD IN *THE PINE KNOT*

—circa 1934

Woman wanted to do
housework.
Finn preferred.

THE COLD

1

It exists.
in January
in Duluth Minnesota
the temperature did not rise above zero
for fourteen days.   fifteen to twenty below
the lows.   zero to minus five the highs.
the sun shined.   the wind slanted.
just off the train
an immigrant
waiting at the depot.   no one came.

2

a Finn.
not much to say.   rather
spend all day bent over a hole chopped in the ice.

3

in November when the temperature first slipped
near zero, it seemed so cold.   the skin seemed
to tremble as if the wind ruled the world and
taxed the skin until it was barren, unable to
sustain.   then temperatures moderated.   snow
fell.   the temperatures fell, actually the air
rose without a cloud cover, but we say fell,
fell back again.   ten below zero.   the cold felt
as if it could not get much colder.   a decree

was read from pulpits throughout the land.   at
twenty below pelts were taxed.   the skin gave
up its fingerbones. they were its white flags
of surrender.   it was much the same at thirty
below. machinery balked.   at forty below
the Russian army stalled outside the capital.
at sixty blow zero the temperature was absolute.
spittle cracked to ice before it hit the snow.
even the air was crystal.   like the ghost found
designed by craftsmen long ago, before the Virgin
Mary traded places with the pagan.

4
it exists.
in a new world
farther to the north
where you can see your breath, a crystal trail
where fear has been.
bright the sun
that never quite
rises beyond horizons.

5
it exists.

FINNS

1

I think of him testifying:
on the seventeenth of January
in the year of our Lord
nineteen hundred and eight
in Duluth Minnesota
before the appointed court
I John Svan swear under oath
that these people
who lived next door to me
were indeed people
Finnish people,
that they were of the fairest of skin,
with eyes that did not slant,
that hair did not grow on their
hands and feet, that they
did not have clawed paws
or make much of the moon,
that they were indeed
people
in the full meaning of the law
so help me God.

2

the sky was overcast.
he read in the *Herald*
that a miner was charged

with stabbing a man
after a card game, they were
friends in Italy, quarreled.
that housework was harder on the
stout woman than her leaner sister.
that a venison dinner came very high
for a section foreman who
regaled his guests with game.
that a late-of-Duluth man is dead,
arrested for being crazy, he died
of diphtheria.   that a La Crosse man
could not be aroused,
lying unconscious for a full week.
that the Pope went to bed with the gout.
that the Giddings Riddance Sale was today.
that the Mattson woman admitted her crime,
said she killed her husband
because he was the devil.
there was guaranteed dentistry.
the marshall too quick
for a Montenegran at McKinley
who pulled his weapon.
a mother claimed her children
just as the humane officer
was about to take them.
there would be no leniency for vags.
another was killed by a drill
in Calumet.   no mention of snow.

3

I think of him thinking:
on the seventeenth of January
in the year of our Lord
nineteen hundred and eight
in Duluth Minnesota
before the appointed court
I John Svan swear under oath
that the snow
which fell this winter past
is the same as the snow
which fell every winter
during every year
of my life in the old country
and that it is indeed
white
in the full meaning of the law
so help me God.

4

although he did not look out his window
he knew it was snowing, felt
the snow touch down on his own.

WOLVES: BETWEEN THE BLACK AND WHITE

Suppose it were November.   near dusk.
        a dust of snow on the ground.
suppose you walked a logging road,
        the road overgrown with popple
        narrowed and became a trail.
suppose a tree had fallen over the trail.
suppose you stepped over it and saw
        the trees move ahead.
suppose a gray shape appeared.
suppose another, beside it.
suppose on your right, five more.
suppose on your left just beyond the trees
        five or six more shapes of gray.
suppose you took a step back and felt
        all the way up your leg
        the fallen log's fur.
suppose the shapes of gray took one step
        toward you.
suppose the shapes of gray had eyes, their stares
        looked that moment into this.
suppose you fired a shot above their heads.
suppose they stayed without a flinch.
suppose you aimed between the leader's eyes
        and fired.
suppose the mate had teeth, snarling.
suppose you aimed again between the eyes
        and fired.

suppose the other shapes disappeared
        as gray becomes the twilight.
suppose up close death were huge.
suppose you carried the heavy fur behind a spruce,
ripped tags from ears, smashed transmitters.
your heart beat thick as six foot popple trees.
suppose you knew somewhere a white cross
        painted on the faded gray boards
        of the door of an outhouse.
suppose you knew.

THE LONE TREE

The way things are
in the middle of every field
on every homestead
a tree
usually a white birch
left only for the birds.
midday
a man wipes his brow
unfolds his lunch
and takes a long slow
swallow of spring water
in the shade of the
uncut tree.
the young like branches
are reaching out
going to town,
leaving home;
there is a girl,
a job in the cities,
then who knows
there are no more letters —
only the fresh cut of hay
rising up,
the sound a baler makes
continuing on, and
the way things are
a tree
left only for the birds.

HARMONY, SOCIAL ORDER, AND THE SOUL ITSELF

An old man
wool shirt buttoned to the top,
fingers missing from one hand,
knuckles red with soreness,
howls a long howl
like that of a wolf,
then cants a good ear
shaped like the last phase of the moon,
and waits.   waits.   at last

from beyond the fringes of firs
a low tremolo
the howling of a wolf,
an older wolf
cut off from the pack
howls for an old man
who listens
with all the hairs in his ears.

the howl starts low
in swampland.
below zero.
it is the longest night of the year
the oldest of legends
the saddest of songs
singers with kanteles
strung with horsehair

ever sang, the only notes
ever written down
were but tracks in the snow.
an old man is like
a white pine uncut all these years,
a stone caught in the roots
exposed in an undercut bank,
or in a machine shed
the blade of a crosscut saw,
on the grease-stained floor
Canadian thistle growing through
the cracked boards,
on a nail well-oiled traps,
in a corner a mason jar
blued and etched with cobwebs.

here an old man
trims the wick
divines water with copper rods
whittles willow flutes
and howls.
an old man uses stone
breaks open the bones
and licks the very marrow.
he eats orts like the wolves
and howls.

WHITE

Nothing was ever as white as the first frost.
the leaves of the birch curled up
were crushed
        dropped, checking the direction of the wind.

nothing was ever as white in northern Minnesota
as the word *Co-op*
now fading from the gray elevator
that squints out over a town, its windows boarded up.

nothing was ever as white as the river that froze
last night. at first the moon gaze was trapped
inside the skim. then degrees fell thicker and thicker,
the river flowing over
as rivers do
forming columns,
and under,
the ice now monumental, closing around all but the last
sigh I know not the origins of,
only that
nothing was ever as white.

nothing was ever as white as the popple trees that have
sprung up in the back forty.
you know how to gypo.
nothing was ever as white.

or stand on a stand all day
thinking the slightest sound should grow into
a large and wary

antlered animal.
the wind cold as a Plymouth.
and your father who worked the mines
had said
if a deer should show
you must not miss.

nothing was ever as white.
nothing ever will be.
nothing will ever be as white
as the wolves no one ever sees.

nothing will be as white as wind-blown snow;
nothing will be as white as the ridges carved from
shadow and hard pack, hollows
striated by whims of wind;
nothing will be as white as one set of tracks
due north
leading on and on
where nothing is.

LOSING THE ANIMAL

Shots shattered November. and bounding by
blood spurting out, an animal.
dressed in red and wanting to be
I followed beneath the concrete bridge
into antlered alder, crashing
always before me.
once I saw the aldered head
on an upbound, then it disappeared.
no tracks, no blood, no fur.
I had even lost sound
of the animal becoming the dusk somewhere.

the morning I searched,
the afternoon on the way out
I found
eyes glazed, dried red splotches,
fur missing — the animal —
shattered leg bone splintered.
when I touched the stiff fur
with my rifle, it did not move.
I cut the skin away with my knife.
bile of a body, bloated jade buddha.
when I cut the flesh . . .
death oozed out
reeking.
even kerosene would not clean

these hands tainted, tainted.
what got in, inside the skin,
into the blood, into the heart —
the animal gone green.

THE ORIGIN OF IRON

So the young man took the old man
whose hair was then white as the foam
          on the lakeshore on a windy day,
showed him the backhoe,
how it ate great mouthful after mouthful
          of earth and roots and clay.

did the young man know the origin of iron.
did he know the old man cut trees
          and built the house (the log house).
did he know the land was as a woman
          dark as the bark of trees on a rainy day.
how the old man plowed the land,
          piled rocks, dug a well.

does a young man look past the end of the road
          at the boughs of the balsam fir.
how the boughs become the trees.
how the stems become the trunks, the flat needles
          the boughs, the boughs shaped
          like the slopes of mountains.
how the roots go down deeper than the cold.
how the water tastes of iron.

THERE WILL BE WILD ROSES ON THE COFFIN

And what words do we know of saying goodbye,
I in the pin-striped suit
I was married in
and you
you in the summer dress
already the wind in the wildflowers.

the bread has been baked,
the pike broiled,
there is beer for the drinking,
coffee sugarlumps and cream,
and wild blueberries in pies,
there are daisies on the table,
a Viola Turpeinen record
plays and plays and plays.

outside the dog is barking.

THE BACK ROADS

Out on the back roads
driven only by road hunters
and others who want only to know
where these roads go,
out on the end of a long-necked pole
anchored to a post or milk pail
filled with cement
an occasional mailbox.
each one
moose-jawed to open and close
take in and spit out
the news of the day.   a red flag
goes up if something to say.
on each is painted a name
like Heinonen.   if you go far enough
you never see anyone.
it is only the balsams that
come out to the road
wanting only to know
who drives these roads.

DOVETAILED CORNERS

Beneath the siding painted white we found
tarpaper, tore it away to preserve
the squared logs, each with dovetailed corners
precisely sawn and with the sweep of an ax
cut into the other lie, corner angle-cut logs
that held all these years. what is left
all else stripped down?
why they came?
the winters long. the summers
short. the moon full.
or the cry of the loon.
the land so rocky. children grew inside
like beetles in the fields,
under the bark of pine, or in their ears.

HUNTERS

Why
in November without snow
does the landscape darken
like the darker fur of wolves.

why in Fond du Lac
does the Chippewa
in his blue and tarpaper shack
lie awake.   he longs for
the wings of a hawk.
the wind creaks through
the cracked window.
his head aches.
his bruised wife lies beside him.
last night he traded in
a rifle.   out back
two Fords and a snowmobile
without a track
have died and rusted to another heaven.

and why in St. Paul
on the legislature steps
the carcass of a wolf?

TREES ARE REMEMBERED AGAIN

In Cass Lake where there is a sign:
RESTAURANT SERVICE STATION WILD RICE
CHIPPEWA GIFT SHOP BINGO;
inside
past wild rice, sweet grass, birch bark baskets;
men at the counter, green pull tabs;
Bear Man saying
"all morning you have been ripping open,
all that work for nothing,
win one now";
farther along
men at the bar
beneath the velvet dancer.

in Ball Club where
mothers man Bah Ga Da Whaning Head Start
and grandmothers weave baskets.

in eastern Montana where
Reindeer Man lost three reindeer,
broke out of the trailer
at 60 m.p.h.
loping across the prairie
antlers broken off.

in Lapland where
television is now

the black and white idol
encircled with
                antlers interlocked.
in the Arctic where
after Chernobyl
hares still feed on snow
                        turn white.

The Reindeer

1

Reindeer live   on moss and such.
you sit on a corral   made of popple logs
watching them.   both cows and bulls
have antlers   which are dark brown
in velvet   throughout the summer.
the fur then   is dark as alder bark
except for the mane   which remains
white as the coming snow
as does a collar   around the hooves.
the average reindeer testicle
weighs 90 grams   in summer
but only 20 grams   in winter.
if you watch them   through the summer
the weight loss is noticeable.

2

when the edges of the maple leaves turn to red
the bucks begin   like a shaman
tossing the head   strips of velvet
hanging from the antlers yet
like snakes   driven from their skins.
snorting at tag alder
snorting at wind.
terrible breath   escapes these nostrils.
the dark firs   only listen.
they have brackets   for ears.
the green swirls   in stagnant waters

know as much   if not more .   of origins.
all depends
on the length of sunlight.

3
it was said
a man who would be a shaman   died
and after a long journey   returned.
some of the better shamans   died many deaths
and always returned.   of course
some of the others   died
and never returned.

it was said
with a mighty sword
a man cut off his leg   then his other leg,
then he cut off an arm   then his head.
other men found him like this
and thinking him dead   buried him.

it was said
a reindeer came to him   in darkness.
he became a raven
and perched on an antlered branch.
they sped away   came to a land of tall trees.
he flew to the tallest of these.
he waited.

4
the fur lightens   becoming nearly white
except for   a dark around the eyes.

winter is   merely absence.
the days grow   shorter and shorter.
restricted   the flow of blood to the legs.
less   the comfort of the cold.
wide hooves scrape away the ice and snow.

5

open the gate.   the great herd moving
moving beyond the trees.
see a man   a man with antlers on his head,
running on all fours   a man with antlers,
a man with antlers   who retrieved the dead,
a man with antlers   who talked to the stones,
got them moving again.

6

reindeer are everywhere.
in these woods
if you leave your body
you must always   return.

THESE ARE MODERN TIMES

A reply made by an Ojibwe guide when told by a judge
he could not use a snowmobile in the Boundary Waters anymore.

Just off the county road
tarpaper
nailed down with strips,
a ladder to the roof where
the roof was shingled years ago,
bleached antlers nailed above
a sliding corrugated door.

deep in grass out back
cars pickup trucks
bodies rusted with sin
and without wheels.
on a popple log tripod
a chain,
the ground around engine-block black.

a rusted bucket
bolts and nails,
a broken chair,
an old shirt hung out on a pump
sleeves limp in the wind
that crossed the field

the next field
green as after rain
where two deer, a doe and fawn,
stand out of the evening.
there they will always be.

SUNDOGS

We know neither
the secret of creation
nor why dogs sleep
on chairs or couches
with knitted throws
around a woodstove
or in the sunlight
their paws chinking in
a part of a life
that wasn't.   once
a man came from
beyond the black spruce
to tell me a chipmunk
passed away.   he
had nothing else to say.
one of the dogs
one with a black mark
over one eye
woke up when he arrived
barked once, then
rolled over.   the first of
January.   minus twelve
degrees.   on the window
there is suddenly so much
sunlight.

HAYING

1

The wind hot.
the year dry.
the hay thin.

the fields cut.   only fifty-five bales (and
it's in the book).
the twenty-seventh of July.   ninety-two in the shade.
faces streaked, black
tractor exhaust, hay dust, sweat.

the Esther Hakkarainen house
large,
the Esther Hakkarainen house
two-storied,
the Esther Hakkarainen house
green-sided, moosehorns by the door.

inside
inside the Esther Hakkarainen house
sat down, at the table
sat down, for coffee.

Esther Hakkarainen saying this was the worst year ever,
Esther Hakkarainen saying she came to this country in 1904,
Esther Hakkarainen saying she was eighty-seven,
Esther Hakkarainen saying she once had six cows, took in
boarders.

Esther Hakkarainen saying she would never sell her land.
not while she was living.   after that
she wouldn't care.
Esther Hakkarainen saying she liked the way
the fields looked when cut.

Esther Hakkarainen saying she didn't want any money,
maybe some hay to put over the septic,
the moosehorns to hold it down.

Esther Hakkarainen picking up the fly swatter, missing.
Esther Hakkarainen saying the flies were small this year,
yesterday she happened to be looking, saw one fly in
through the keyhole.

outside
outside the Esther Hakkarainen house
the wind hot.
the year dry.
the sky darkening in the west.

2

the road into the late Charlie Mattson's field is rough, the road
the late Charlie Mattson used to walk to town everyday.   Charlie
Mattson never drove.   after a few beers one night, a little
confused, found an open door and went to sleep.   townspeople
now lock their doors.

in Charlie Mattson's field
a log barn
gray and leaning in.

in Charlie Mattson's field
the wind.
in Charlie Mattson's field
a shed collapsed.   half-sawn logs, old mattress, brown
whiskey bottles, rusted Hamm's cans.
in Charlie Mattson's field
inevitably raspberries.

once people at the bar thought Charlie Mattson smelled a little
strong, took up a collection, bought him clothes.   the next day at
the bar, Charlie Mattson, same old clothes.   someone asked if he
liked the clothes.   Charlie Mattson said he liked them fine.
Charlie Mattson who will always be Charlie Mattson.   then, on
the first day of June, Charlie Mattson, new shirt buttoned to the
top, cuffed trousers.   everyone was always asking so many
questions, no use to save them.   Charlie Mattson, who the next
time he changed his clothes, thought he ought to wear them.

in Charlie Mattson's field
a sauna.
squared logs, greasy brown, dovetailed corners.
the door a chrome car door handle.
the hinges trapezoidal.
between the dressing room and steam
a window broken.   the sill a shelf
where once a lantern stood.

in Charlie Mattson's field
the house burned down.   the foundation stones.
a deer dead.

in Charlie Mattson's field
in the far side of a hill
a root cellar.

open the door.   the air cool, of the earth.
open another door.   there
sitting on a bench, Charlie Mattson.
Charlie Mattson saying he liked the way the field looked
when cut.
Charlie Mattson saying it is no use letting it go into the trees.
all the years spent clearing, hauling rocks.
close the door.   the other door.
brace it with a log.

by the road, at the blacktop, a stop sign. no one knows
why it was ever there.

in Charlie Mattson's field
the hay thin.
in Charlie Mattson's field
the wind.
the trees beyond the field.

A FISH STORY

In a yellowed photograph I am five years old
and standing beside a huge fish, a northern pike.
its mouth is slightly open like enormous pliers.
there is a rope strung through the trap-like gills
from which the fish hangs from a willow limb
I used to climb out onto. when I asked,
my father said the fish was twenty-six pounds
and fourteen ounces and that he would have caught
that fish except that one Hjalmer Maki, the man
who caught the fish on a daredevil, wouldn't stop
the boat when my father yelled to him against the
wind to stop the boat, that he had hooked a big fish,
but the lake was too rough and Hjalmer Maki
wouldn't shut the motor off. my father said he
must have fought that fish for half an hour
while Hjalmer Maki and his Johnson three horse
kept on puttputtputt into the big wind until
finally the fish got off. for weeks Hjalmer Maki
trolled alone before he caught the big fish and
my father swore it was from the same spot he had
hooked his big fish so it must have been the same
fish. now every summer the lake turns green.

LIVING IN POPULATION UNKNOWN

Only October
and it snowed.
a one-legged crow perched on the wire.
bear tracks across the yard.
the dogs asleep on the sofa
in the chairs around the woodstove.
the cats walk on the table.
the kids, both in their teens, have gone to town.
you, being the last farmer in Finland Minnesota,
go too once a week

for feed. only yesterday
a woman at the Co-op saying
logging doesn't cut it anymore
that she's going back to the cities.
the cows need milking.
the chickens are for eggs.
you don't know what the horses are for.
a coyote should be released.
the reindeer live on a piece of alder ground

you built a fence around.
down the road lives your wife's mother.
last Thursday she baked and, as reported
in the county chronicle,
seven ladies came to visit.
coffee, biscuit, pieces of cake
were what she served.   an aunt

lives in the huge house
with the second story closed off.
over the kitchen is a carved ceiling

no one has ever seen.
a cousin lives farther on
in a house surrounded with grass
all summer she forgot to mow.
there you saw the daisies explode.
another saw Jesus
rise from the cream
and didn't think she had to pay.
another grows Xmas trees

and knows how to gypo.
the sun melts the tracks across the yard but
you know
how long it takes to sort out the now.
the woman at the Co-op,
who wasn't your wife's cousin, has gone
where the paychecks come once a week.

here the winter so early
white moths rise up
out of the snow.

The Visit

You must not be late.   spit your snoose
out (if you chew) into the snow.   at the
door take off your boots even if your host
tells you you do not need to.   his family
will have placed theirs neatly on the braided
rag rug by the door.   place yours there also.
many who visit bring along wool socks to
wear on linoleum floors.

inside sit down as the host directs.   be
careful not to sit in his chair.   in the
living room it will be the one that has
the crumpled knitted throw, or in the
kitchen it will be the one not squarely
facing the table like all the others but
will be slightly askew.   after sitting
down do not talk of grown sons or daughters
or socialism or the mines.   instead talk
of wooden spoons of moonlight or of frogs.
do not pretend to know all about these things.

eventually the hostess will announce that
coffee will be served.   it is considered
rude to serve coffee too soon.   but if it
is not served after a reasonable time a
guest may wonder what time it is or switch
the conversation to milking or the chickens.

the table will be spread with biscuit
and breads and pieces of cake and cookies.
coffee will be served in the finest cups
either from the old country or from the
Miller Hill Mall. there will be a bread
and butter plate, a cup and saucer, and
a small spoon. there will be a bowl of
sugar lumps, a pitcher of cream (bachelors
may serve Carnation milk from a can with
two holes pegged with wooden pegs), and
a vase of lilacs, wild roses, daisies,
or violets.

when the hostess pours the first cup of
coffee take a piece of the biscuit, with
the second cup take a piece of unfrosted
cake, and with the third either a piece
of berry pie or a piece of fancy frosted
cake. a fourth cup may be taken with
cookies or a sugar lump (sipping coffee
from a saucer with a lump of sugar held
between the teeth is acceptable if you
are used to doing this at home) or
whatever else has not been tasted. it
is better to take too much than too little
making sure all items have been tasted.

after coffee it will be time to leave.
tell the host and hostess the coffee pot
is always on at your house. but for now

there are many chores to do and our lives
are so short and it is a pity we must always
be in such a hurry and it is too bad we
are not all rich.

HEAD CHEESE

We eat the heart,
      the throat
      the brains, sliced a mosaic remains,
we use all of the animal.

we break open the bones,
lick the narrow marrow,
eat the very tongue, and
use all of the animal.

skins stretched for drying,
sinews split for thread,
bones carved, then worshipped,
we use all of the animal.

knife twisted into the heart,
blood flowing into the stomach
now removed in moonlight,
we use all of the animal.

fresh blood in pancakes,
first milk in cheese,
a little *viili*,
we use all of the animal.

there are scratch marks on trees,
the bushes trampled,
black shit
pitted with chokecherry seeds.

what we are we are:
Finns,
Italians,
Serbs and Indians,
even Swedes.   what we are

we are.   we use all
all of the animal.

GETTING THE COWS

At dusk go down the hill
                          through the maples
into the hayfield
where the cows are grazing.
count them
            eight
                  to be sure.
and something else
                  on the ground.
the bull standing broadly by,
horns out like a man's hands
showing how big a fish he caught.
a cow licking a calf
                    a calf!
brown and curly as the bull.
other cows grazing nearby.
go back up the hill
                    through the maples
into the hayfield.
roll the calf over
                  wet and warm
a heifer calf
a heifer calf to build a herd.
spray the red and severed umbilical.
lift the calf into the wheelbarrow.
push her up the hill
                    through the maples

toward the barn.
the cow walking at your side
afterbirth hanging from her valley,
remember chokecherries in a plastic bag.
the calf tries to get up,
put her back down.
she has pissed her hay
                    wet and warm
but has to lie in it.
other cows
        calves
        bull
following close behind
going home: a birthday procession.
up the hill
            through the maples
back to the barn. already dark.

On the Common and Individual
Development of Form

I

The sauna stands a small log building
by the shore of a northern lake
now calm and thoroughly relaxed
in the long shadows of evergreens.
woodsmoke lingers in the air.
inside, a woodstove.   on it
rocks taken from the lakeshore.
someone has painted a sign: *if too hot*
throw water onto the rocks
and nailed it to a log wall.
high on wooden benches,
the nails recessed,
the old sat in two hundred degrees
of steam and forty watt light
switching their naked bodies with switches
made of birch.   they spoke a language
that came from across the Urals
guided only by the Great Bear —
exact routes lost long ago,
routes we can no longer put to tongue,
routes snowed in and silent.

2

before Gustavus Wasa
even Jesus was born in a sauna.
on a Saturday night
first a father, his father, uncles, sons
(one went to school, one ran a trapline,
another drew, drew what no one else could understand),
and a brother-in-law who knew him and him
and every who who was no good . . .
later a mother, aunts, daughters (one was married
to a minister, the other wasn't),
and a mother-in-law who knew
who was who and who was too good for whom. . . .
in each rock a fire was lit.
the water died, rose again from the rock.

3

now
it is midsummer when I run from the sauna
out onto the end of the dock
and jump

        into the waters
        cold and dark as Asia.

What a Lake Is

I

A lake is for seeing
the sunrise orange and abstract
as it lightens into sky.
when the wind and waves roll
over and fall back
and become another,
end at one end
and begin again at the other.
how the trees bow.   mostly fir
and white pine.
how they straighten.   their
reflections grown
of the same roots.

2

the nights bright
distilled with stars,
without wind, when
the cry of the loon
seems to quibble,
spread itself out across a lake
like waves,
is of the reeds,
is sometimes wacky, even
up on wings; in the true North
and only the north is true

it is the morning of one who has
gone away.

3

when I look long into a lake
the water so clear
it only keeps on going,
like the white pines
or northern lights or
the howl of a wolf, it keeps on going.
water grows
both ways:
                    into knowing,
into not.   think of winter

4

when a lake turns over in its sleep
and screams.

5

once I held you like a lake.

PIKE

Think of weeds
thick with teeth
long thin horizontal weeds
even more green
          slippery scaled
more slippery than black water.

the sun rising
beyond the dead firs.
birds chirping.
a deer lapping at
the water colored pond.

the sunlight slanting into green;
spring evolved from a pike's dream.
mottled clouds like spotted skin
even scales
all a summer's day.

call it *hauki*.   call it jack.
ancient out of algae
it grows teeth.   almost as easy
it grows length.   almost as easy
it grows girth.   almost as ancient
it grows teeth.   call it pike.

except for northern pike
the smaller anything is
the better.   once

E. Jarvinen hammered out a spoon.
how it caught pike.
many thought it illegal.   when
in his sleep
old Jarvinen died
his secret within him.

be careful.
a slash of hand
treble hooks driven deep inside
blood stitching from the skin.

in a photo
E. Jarvinen on a rainy day.
from a tree
three pike strung through the gills
like blacks
                hung from a lamp post
in Duluth.   in the mines

Finns were listed black.
leeches are the lake's mosquitos.
there are devil fish too.
the Ojibwe say
Jesus cast a silver spoon
with treble hooks.
a wind came up.

on a black day
fish for pike
on a lake that has no bottom.
fish for pike
with spoons.   red and white
flashing bright
inside the y-bones of a pike.

once
on a red and white daredevil
I caught a pike,
hung it from a pine tree,
hung it from a limb.
on a tree limb
the pike sang to me.
it sang.
it sang.
from its jaws an epic flowed.
old and steadfast were its jaws.
after thirty summers
and thirty winters
broken on a reef:

        heaven and earth
        stars and moon and sky.

the pike still sings.
minus the fillets
only head backbone tail
it sings.   from its gills
it still sings.

in an old woman's soup its sings.
in E. Jarvinen's sleep its sings.
true leader of the cooperative movement
it sings.
teeth marks on a Rapala
it sings.
and what about the y-bones? it sings.
in your throat
it sings.
it sings.

OPENING DAY

No boat.
no motor.
no locater.   caught
a fish off the dock.
after dark caught a fish.
three times
that what was in me
turned back into the depths,
then held.
darkness weakened.
netted two large eyes
the moon's reflections.
lifted shape and weight
a fish
a large fish
        onto the dock.
shined a light,
the fish grew larger.

in the morning
the fish grew larger yet.
cut thick scales the belly.
the children watched.
pulled out the vitals.
can I touch?
cut off the head.
can I touch?
and nailed the head to a tree.
facing east.
what for?
laid bread beneath the tree.
what for?
on my knees
prayed, forgive me.

WOLVES

I

Morning
and not a whimper.
the moon chill
had scattered frost across the near fields.

when I found the dog dead
dead at the end of the frozen chain
I blew blew blew
until the ghost entered the clasp
and unfroze it at last,
as if my breath could bring back
life. it couldn't.
the throat ripped
the abdomen tore open
the dog was dead.

unclasped
what remained
was of the wolves
fur
flesh
and bone
   warm yet as the stars
over a bent over earth
white with fright.

2

against the chill
I loaded the woodstove
pulled on wool melton pants
pockets that sagged with
cartridges
matches
and wire
a cache of head cheese and biscuit
a jar of gonads.

then
looked long into
the oiled gleam
of rifling.
night after night
raven after raven
scavenged the reddened flesh
the crushed bone.
furborn or not
inside was ancient hatred —
a bullet was light
at the end of the blueblack night.

this was tempered
made in the U.S.A.
steel,
eight cartridges,
opened and closed
one was for the chamber —
a dog lay dead.

3
for a moment,
among the dark humus dripping
roots
strewn with
bones feathers fur
here where sniff was history,
I prepared
teeth to each
paw pad and claw.

4
the trees had surrendered
their leaves.
I walked

all day against the wind   the sky clouded over
no sign of wolves   eight dogs were dead   if only
I had waited   each night with a rifle   waited
for eyes knotting the shadows of birches
night after night my own eyes splintered open
by death smell and deer hair blown across
an April five years ago   a deer unable to get up
onto the blood splashed crust   flesh and hair
snapped from its broken down flanks   then ears
bristling   fierce lined eyes and teeth turned
at me   I walked away   this death becoming
the moment of my own
the dusk upon me
I turned
in wet clay and

track on my track
a wolf!
a four-toed ace of spades
a track as large
as nearly half my own.

5
traps.
one Oedipus Koski
a wolfer
and I tried traps —
the civilized 14 Newhouse
buried for weeks
boiled in bark water
smeared in tallow
all to give a black odor.

we set each
with a five foot chain
and grapple
near a tainted bait,
covered with leaves, dried grass.
we waited. . . .

6
I waited.
on still cloudless nights
complete with moon
I heard them howl
that low

louder
ever melancholy howl
that hackled the hair along my back.

first at one end of the frozen lake
howling
then at the other end
howling howling
near the point
and across
howling howling the unchained howling.

7
it was thirty-one below zero
the night a Finn woman
looked out
and saw nothing
but the stars.
yet she knew
        a massive skull
        its pelage thick
        and nearly white
was there,
where in the morning
there were no tracks.

8
wolves are seldom seen
yet always there —
deer hair
crushed bone
blood streaked April snow.

9

the rafters of the barn
are chinked with sunlight,
I watch the sky,
the laws the rivers
flow into backwaters,
in the evenings
I take out my teeth,
the Winchester
always above the door.

10

it has come to this:
these entrails
set out
and covered with brush
where a wolf
once so distant
circles
in ever narrowing circles,
a wolf that haunts the forest
a wolf seldom seen
        yet always there
a wolf that howls within us
a wolf that leaves no tracks.

Notes to the Poems

"Rune" is an old Finnish word for poem.

"The History of Finland, Minnesota": The historical account is from Hans Wasatjerna's *The History Of Finns In Minnesota*.

"The Cold": After the turn of the century so many immigrants who came to northern Minnesota, Wisconsin, and Michigan waited at the depot in Duluth for a train to take them inland, a room was built, set aside: The Immigrant Room.

"Finns": "Finns were ineligible for citizenship based on a series of Oriental Exclusion Acts. On January 4, 1908, Svan and sixteen other Finns were denied citizenship by District Attorney John C. Sweet of St. Paul. However, on January 17 of that same year, Judge William A. Cant of the U.S. District Court sitting in Duluth officially declared that though perhaps Finns had been 'Mongols' in the remote past their blood had been so tempered by that of the Teutonic and other races that they 'are now among the whitest people in Europe.'" – Inkeri Väänänen-Jensen.

"Harmony, Social Order, and the Soul Itself": A kantele is a stringed instrument played by Finnish singers. Many of the older songs were collected in the *Kalevala*, the national epic.

"Orts" is a word my father used. It could be of Eskimo or Finnish origin or maybe from "aorta." It means "innards."

"White": Blacklisted for trying to organize other mineworkers, many Finnish socialists joined the American Communist Party headed for many years by Gus Hall of Cherry, Minnesota. To *gypo* is to buy at a lower price, usually pulpwood or Christmas trees, and then sell at a higher price, a form of capitalism.

"The Lone Tree": In the *Kalevala*, Väinämöinen, when he had cleared the land for pasture, was said to have left one tree for the birds.

"On the Common and Individual Development of Form": *Sauna* is pronounced with an "ow" as in "too hot."

"Head Cheese": *Viili* is a Finnish yogurt made with whole milk.

"Pike": *Hauki* is a Finnish word for Pike.

JIM JOHNSON was born in Cloquet, Minnesota, and has lived all of his life in northern Minnesota. Since 1973, Johnson has taught in the Duluth public schools. He currently teaches at Denfeld High School. Jim Johnson's work has been published in *The Beloit Poetry Journal*, *Kansas Quarterly*, and *Finnish Americana*, and has been anthologized in *Sampo: The Magic Mill* (New Rivers Press) and *Mixed Voices* (Milkweed Editions). Jim Johnson's first book, *Finns in Minnesota Midwinter*, was published by North Star Press in 1986.